UNDERSTANDING DISEASE AND WELLNESS

Kids' Guides to Why People Get
Sick and How They Can Stay Well

A KID'S GUIDE TO OBESITY

VILLAGE EARTH PRESS

Series List

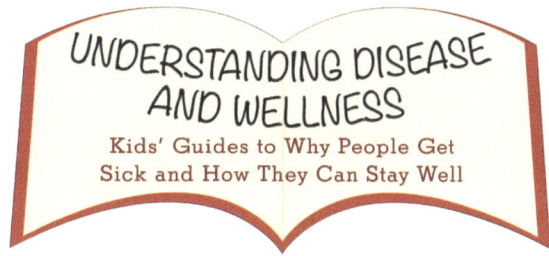

A KID'S GUIDE TO OBESITY

Sheila Stewart

Understanding Disease & Wellness:
Kids' Guides to Why People Get Sick and How They Can Stay Well
A KID'S GUIDE TO OBESITY

Village Earth Press
Vestal, NY 13850
www.villageearthpress.com

First Printing

9 8 7 6 5 4 3 2 1

Series ISBN (paperback): 978-1-62524-445-1
ISBN (paperback): 978-1-62524-417-8
ebook ISBN: 978-1-62524-052-1
    Library of Congress Control Number: 2013911245

Author: Sheila Stewart.

Produced by Vestal Creative Services.
www.vestalcreative.com

Introduction

According to a recent study reported in the Virginia Henderson International Nursing Library, kids worry about getting sick. They worry about AIDS and cancer, about allergies and the "super-germs" that resist medication. They know about these ills—but they don't always understand what causes them or how they can be prevented.

Unfortunately, most 9- to 11-year-olds, the study found, get their information about diseases like AIDS from friends and television; only 20 percent of the children interviewed based their understanding of illness on facts they had learned at school. Too often, kids believe urban legends, schoolyard folktales, and exaggerated movie plots. Oftentimes, misinformation like this only makes their worries worse. The January 2008 *Child Health News* reported that 55 percent of all children between 9 and 13 "worry almost all the time" about illness.

This series, **Understanding Disease and Wellness**, offers readers clear information on various illnesses and conditions, as well as the immunizations that can prevent many diseases. The books dispel the myths with clearly presented facts and colorful, accurate illustrations. Better yet, these books will help kids understand not only illness—but also what they can do to stay as healthy as possible.

—*Dr. Elise Berlan*

Just the Facts

- Obesity means having too much fat on your body.

- Obesity is a big problem around the world for people who are young and old, rich and poor. It is a health problem more than a "looks" problem. Obesity can cause many different illnesses.

- Your doctor can find out if you are obese or overweight by measuring your body mass index (BMI).

- Obesity is caused by eating more calories than you burn off by being active.

- Exercising and eating right are two ways you can take care of yourself. You're worth the effort!

What Is Obesity?

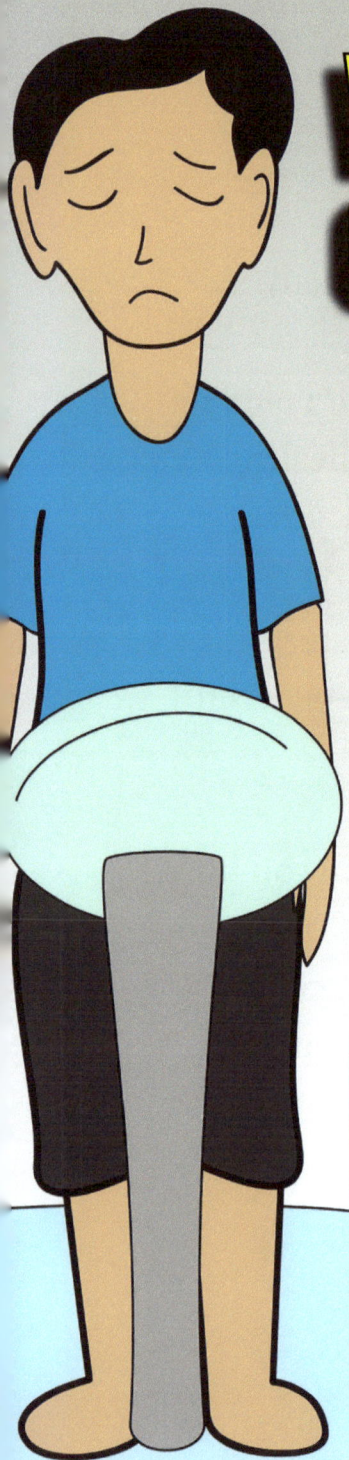

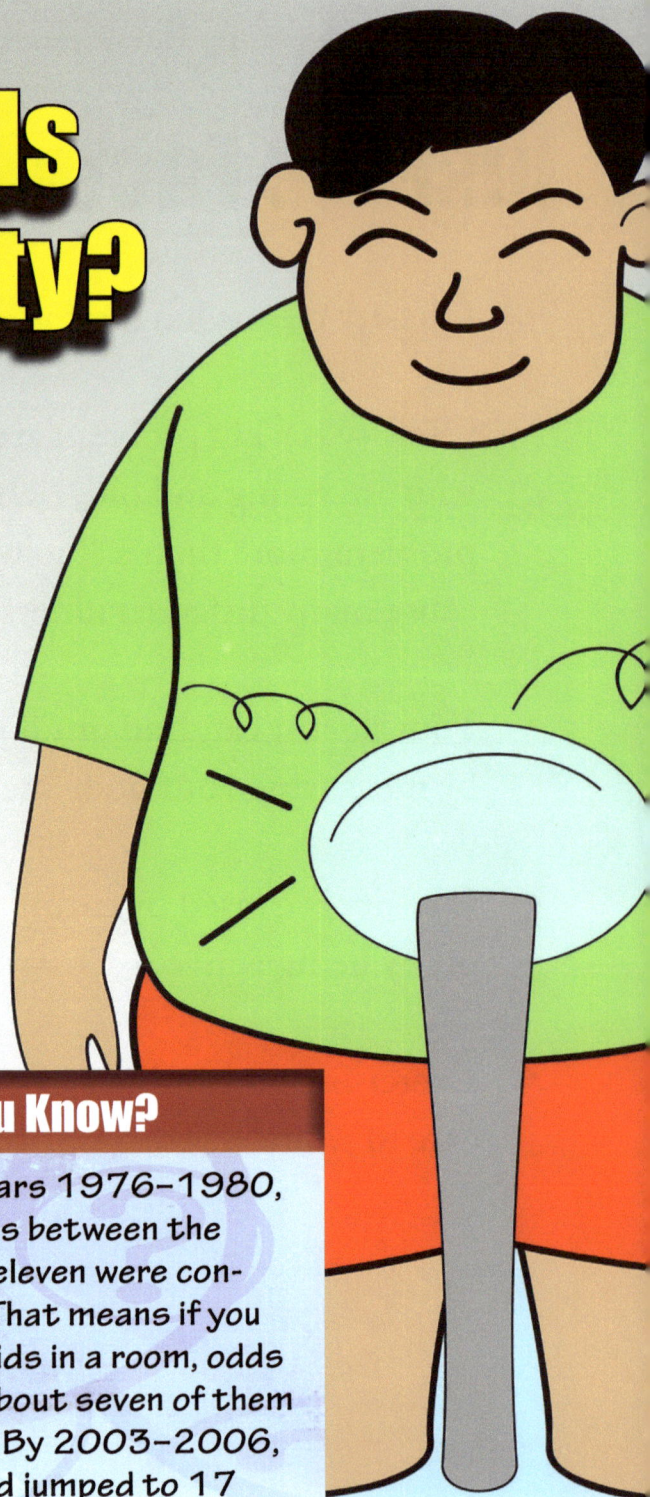

Obesity means having too much body fat. Obesity isn't about how a person looks, though. When a person is obese, his body fat makes him unhealthy.

How much a person weighs is only one part of being obese. Doctors also look at how tall a person is and what her body type is. They also look at her BMI (*body mass index*). If her BMI is higher than 95 percent of other people the same age, doctors say she is obese. If it is between 85 and 95 percent, she is overweight.

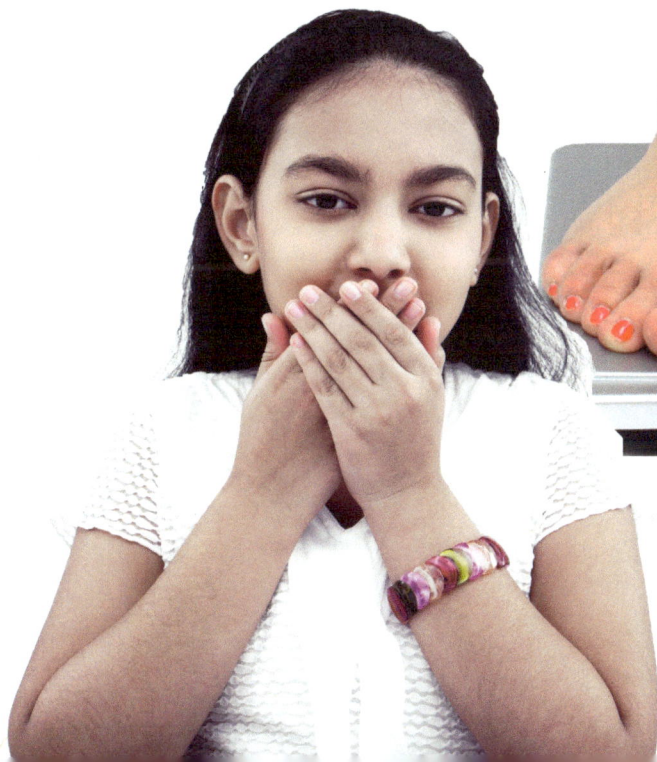

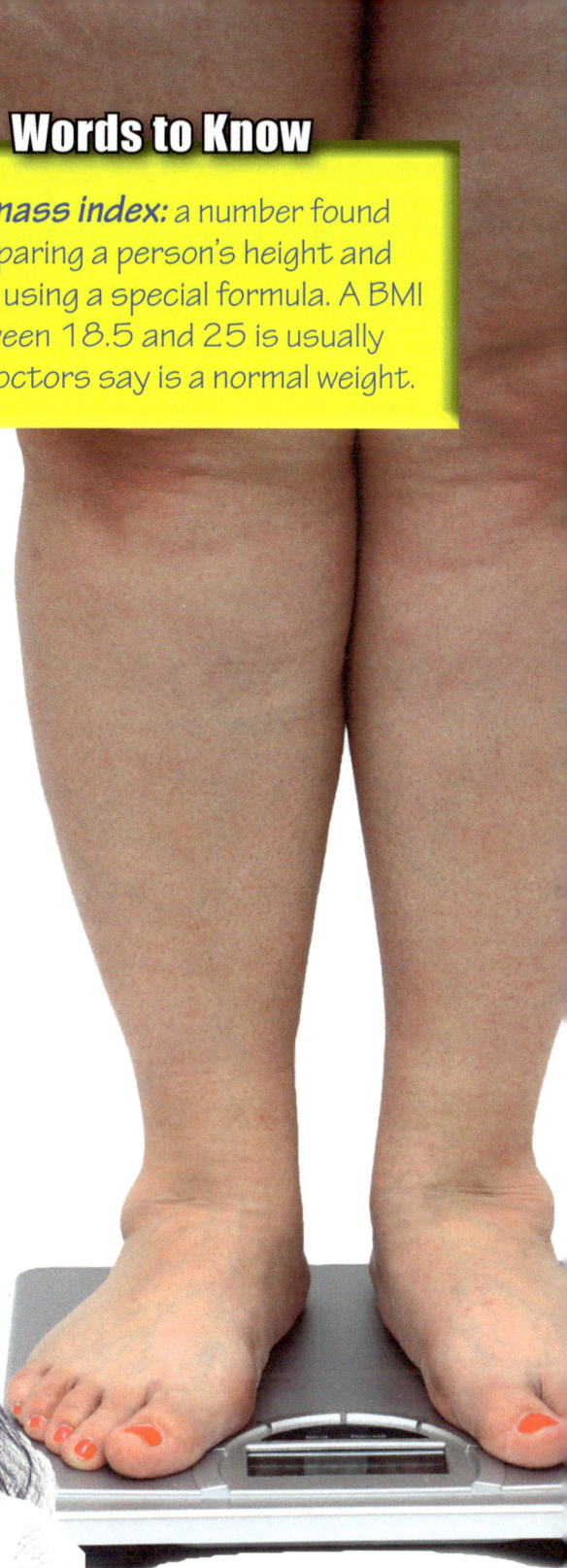

A Big Problem

All over the world, obesity rates are rising. In 2005, 400 million adults were obese. By 2015, doctors and scientists think around 700 million will be obese. A lot of children are becoming obese as well. In 2005, 20 million children under the age of five were obese.

People used to think that obesity was just a problem in *developed countries*. But that's not true. *Developing countries* have a lot of overweight and obese people, too, especially in the cities. While some people don't have enough to eat in these countries, others eat lots of cheap, unhealthy food.

Obesity is a big problem for people of all ages and people all over the world.

Words to Know

Developed countries: countries with more factories and other businesses, where most people make more money and have more belongings.

Developing countries: countries with fewer industries and other businesses, where most people are poor.

Did You Know?

Obesity is a big health problem, but being overweight isn't healthy either. And millions more people are overweight. By 2015, more than 2 billion people around the world will probably be overweight!

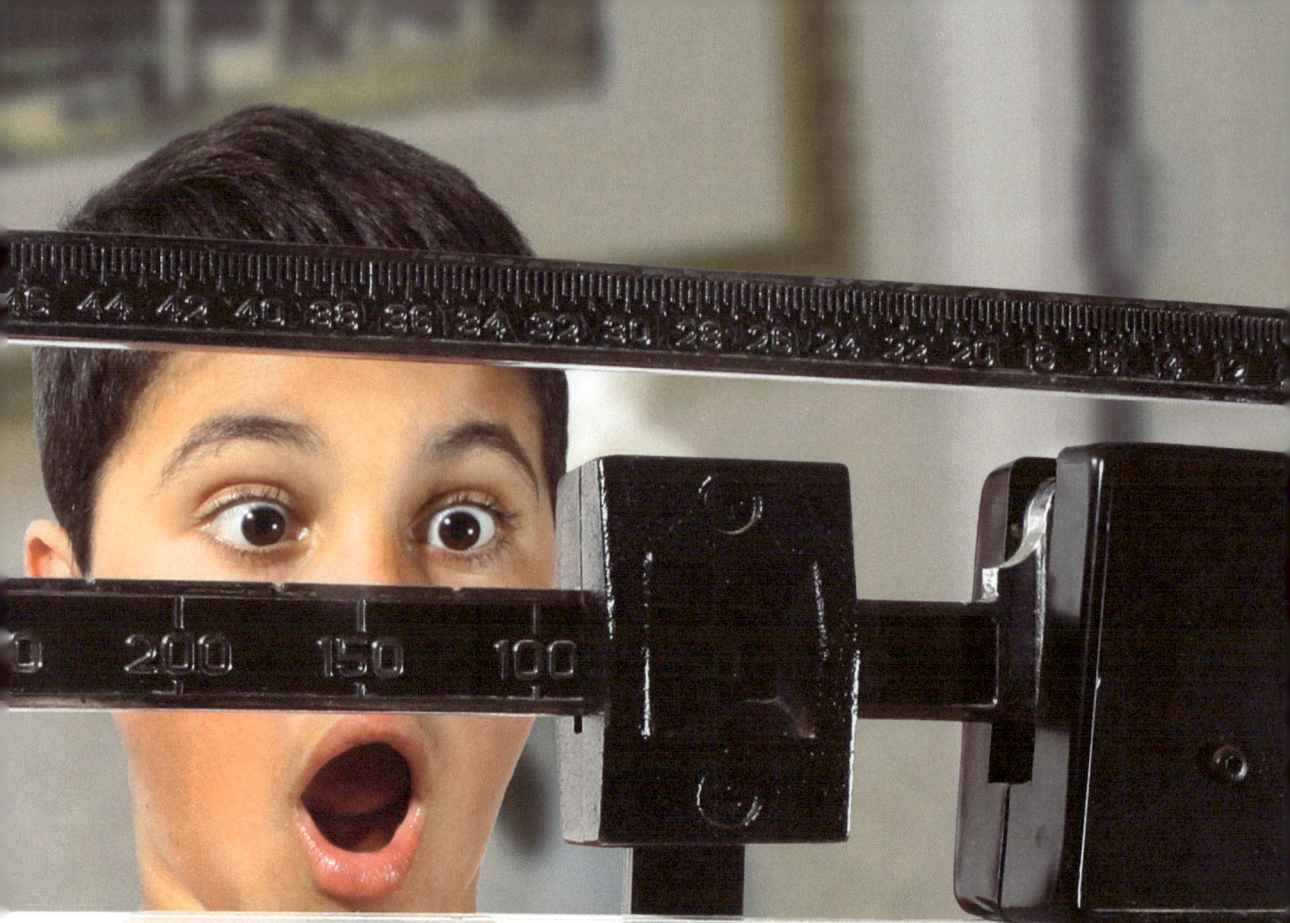

How Do You Know If You Weigh Too Much?

If your clothes are getting tight, it doesn't always mean you're getting fat. You're probably just growing. Kids grow out of their clothes all the time. It's a normal part of being a kid.

Because kids are growing all the time, though, you might have trouble knowing if you do weigh too much. Your doctor can help you figure that out. First, she'll weigh you and measure how tall you are. Then, she'll do some math to figure out what your BMI is. That will tell her if your weight is in the normal range.

Your doctor might also do a special "*pinch test*" to see how much fat you have on certain parts of your body.

Words to Know

Pinch test: the body fat pinch test is done with a special piece of equipment, called calipers, to measure the thickness of fat. Doctors usually measure fat at places like your upper arm, your waist, and your thigh.

How Does Obesity Make You Sick?

Having too much body fat—being obese—is very hard on your body. When you have more weight to carry around, every part of your body has to work harder. That might be okay if you were getting a lot of exercise and all that weight was from muscles. *Athletes* sometimes weigh a lot, but they are not obese. Their weight comes from muscles instead of fat.

Obesity takes a lot of energy. If you have extra weight, you might not feel like moving around as much or as quickly. But your body NEEDS to move around. Usually, if you are obese, you are also *out of shape*. Your heart might start to have trouble pumping your blood, you might feel like you're out of breath a lot, and your hips and knees might ache. Obesity makes it harder to do the things you really want to do.

Words to Know

Athletes: people who train their bodies to play sports or exercise.

Out of shape: not physically fit; not able to work or play easily without getting tired.

Diabetes and Obesity

Diabetes is a disease where your body is unable to handle sugar the way it needs to. In type 1 diabetes, a person's body stops making *insulin*. In type 2 diabetes, on the other hand, your body still makes insulin, but it stops being able to use it. Type 2 diabetes is often caused by being overweight and not getting enough exercise.

Diabetes is a serious disease. Not having enough insulin, or not using it, means your body can't use sugar as energy. Instead, the sugar in your blood gets in the way of other things your body is supposed to do. Having untreated diabetes can cause kidney problems, blindness, and numbness in your fingers and toes.

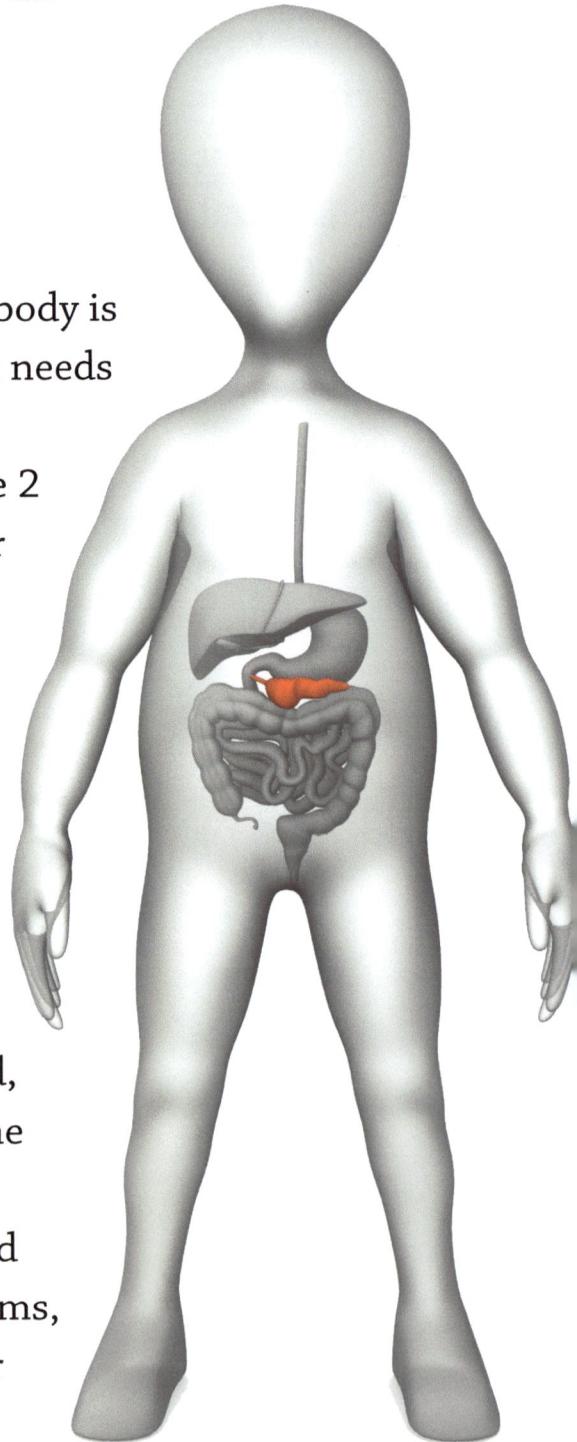

Words to Know

Insulin: a chemical made by your body that lets your cells take in sugar to use as energy. Insulin is made by your pancreas, the organ that is shown as orange in the picture on the facing page.

Did You Know?

If you have diabetes, you may need to have your blood tested every day to see what your blood sugar levels are. The machine in this picture takes a drop of blood from the girl's finger and tests it for sugar.

Asthma and Obesity

Did You Know?

Obesity can make inflammation worse. Fat cells produce certain chemicals that make swelling more likely. This can lead to different diseases, including asthma. People with asthma often need to take medicine through an inhaler (like the one the girl is using on the facing page) to reduce the swelling.

Asthma is a disease that causes *inflammation* in your *airways*. A lot of different things, like pollution or allergies, can cause asthma or make it worse. Being obese can also make you more likely to get asthma. If you are overweight, your lungs have to work harder to push your chest out to breathe. People who are obese sometimes have to take smaller breaths. That means not as much air is getting into their lungs. And that can make asthma worse.

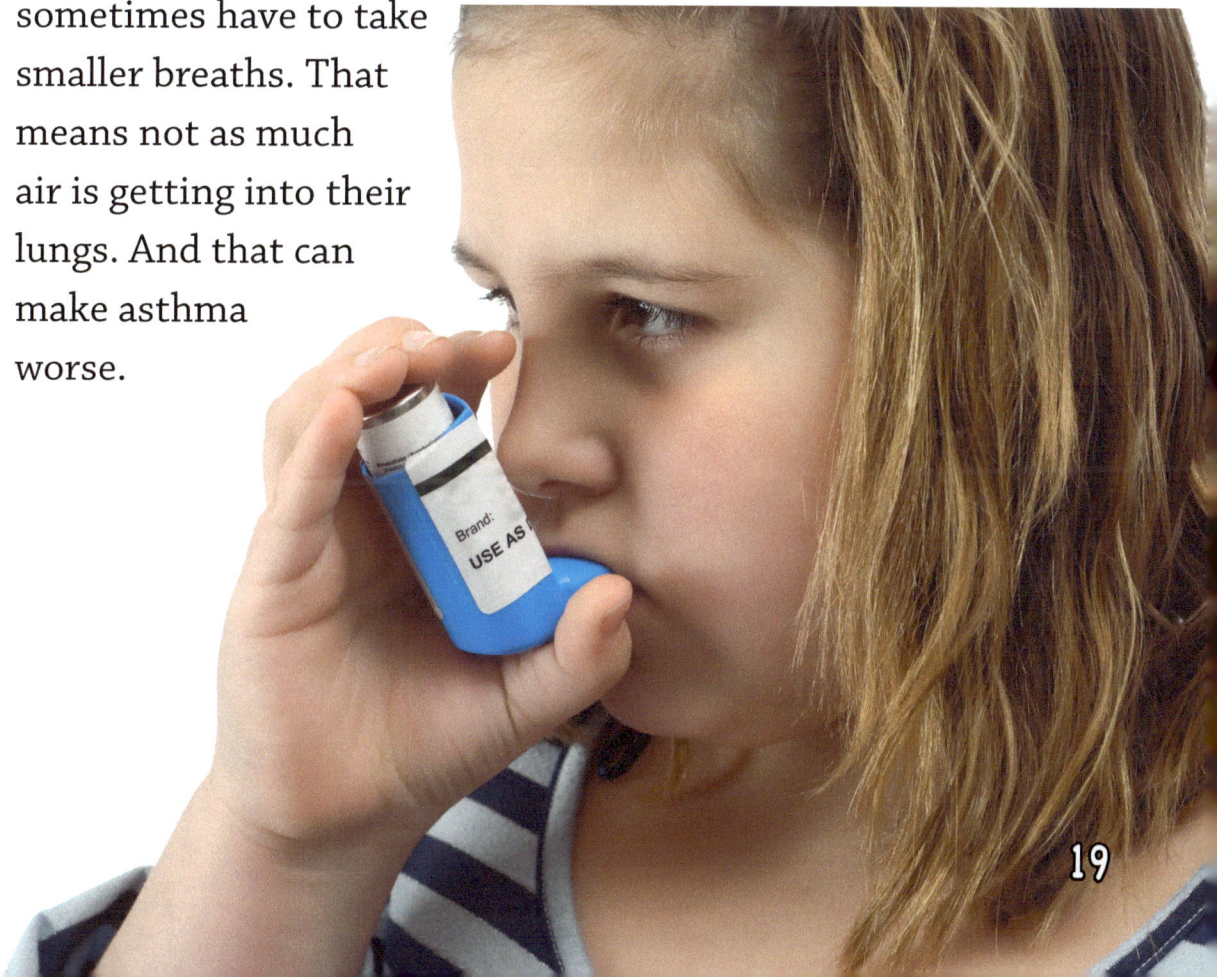

High Blood Pressure and Obesity

Did You Know?

High blood pressure doesn't usually cause symptoms—unless it is very, very high—but it can make your heart or kidneys not work the way they should. Doctors use a device like the one shown on the facing page to measure your blood pressure.

Imagine water flowing through a hose. Your blood flowing through your blood vessels is a little like that. If the water pressure is high, it can be hard on the hose. In the same way, if your blood pressure is high, it can be hard on your blood vessels.

A person's blood pressure could be high because he has too much blood pumping through his blood vessels. This can happen if your heart is beating faster than usual or working harder. Blood pressure can also be high if your blood vessels are too narrow.

Obesity can make your blood pressure high in both these ways. If you have too much fat, your body makes more of certain chemicals. A little of these chemicals are fine, and even healthy, but too much may cause problems. Some of these chemicals make your heart beat faster, making it pump more blood. Others make your blood vessels stiffer and tighter.

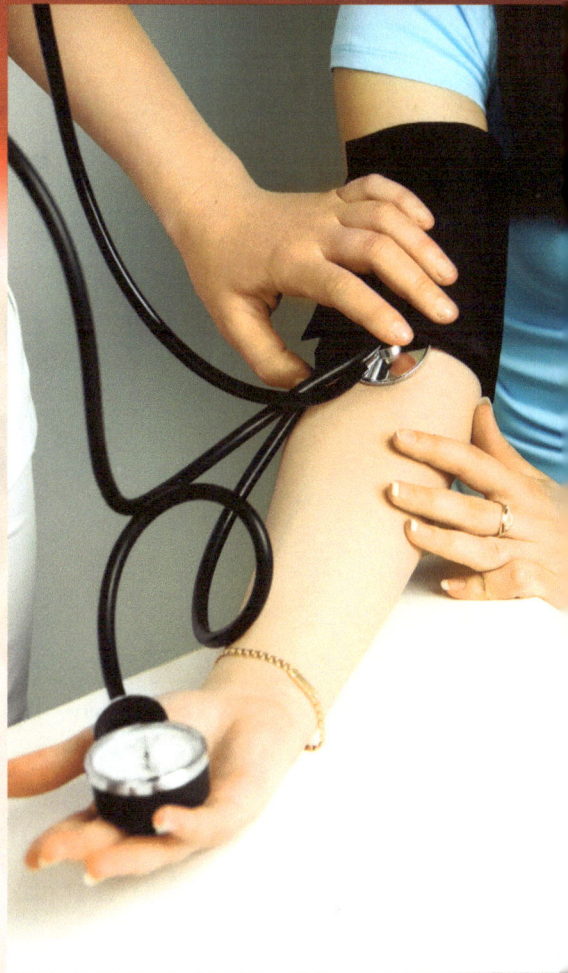

Heart Disease and Obesity

Obesity puts a lot of strain on your heart. Having a bigger body means you have more blood, so your heart has to work harder. At the same time, being overweight can lead to high *cholesterol*. Cholesterol builds up along the inside of your *arteries*, making it harder for the blood to get through. If an artery gets blocked completely, part of the heart can't get enough oxygen and it stops working. This is a heart attack.

Sometimes, obesity puts so much strain on a person's heart that the heart gets tired. It might not be able to keep a regular rhythm of beats, or it might stop altogether.

Words to Know

Cholesterol: a type of fat made naturally by your body and found in other foods. Cholesterol can stick to the insides of your blood vessels and clog them up.

Arteries: the main blood vessels carrying blood away from your heart to the rest of your body.

My uncle is really overweight, but he seems just fine. Does obesity *always* cause health problems?

A: Even if your uncle is healthy right now, his weight means he has a greater risk of developing health problems in the future. Being obese is a risk factor for many different kinds of diseases. Losing even 5 or 10 percent of his body weight (10 or 20 lbs for a 200 lb person— or 4.5 to 9 kg for a 90 kg person) will decrease his health risks.

23

Stroke and Obesity

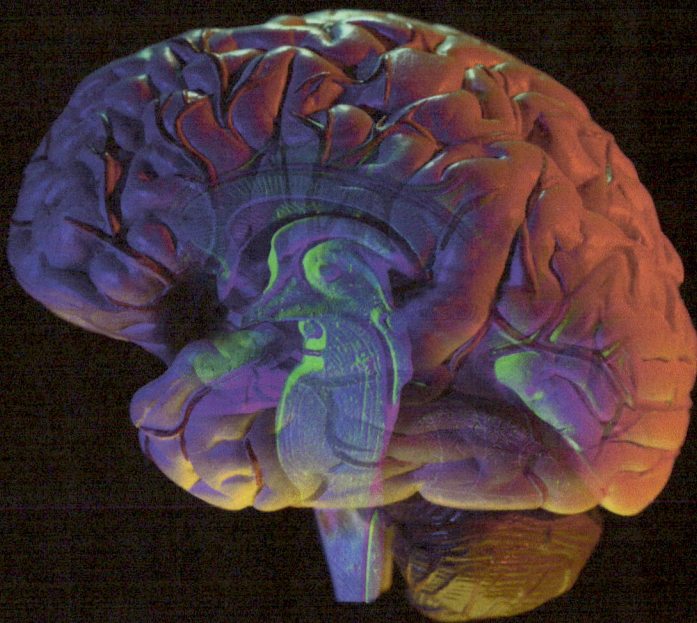

Words to Know

Nutrients: the chemicals your cells use for food.

Paralysis: not being able to move your muscles.

A stroke happens when blood can't reach part of your brain. Since your brain needs the oxygen and *nutrients* in the blood to work properly, it starts to die as soon as the blood supply is cut off. Depending on which part of the brain is dying, and how quickly the person gets medical help, a stroke could lead to speech problems, *paralysis*, or death.

Strokes happen either because a blood vessel gets blocked and the blood can't get through, or because a blood vessel develops a leak. (Remember the water hose we talked about on page 21?)

People who are obese have a higher risk of both types of stroke. Obesity makes cholesterol buildup in blood vessels more likely, which increases the risk of stroke, as well as the risk of heart attacks and heart disease. Obesity also increases the risk of high blood pressure. Since having high blood pressure means the blood is pushing harder through your arteries, this raises the risk that a blood vessel will start to leak. People who are obese are more than twice as likely to have a stroke as someone whose weight is in the normal range.

Kids don't usually have strokes, but kids who are obese are at a much higher risk of a stroke as they get older.

Cancer and Obesity

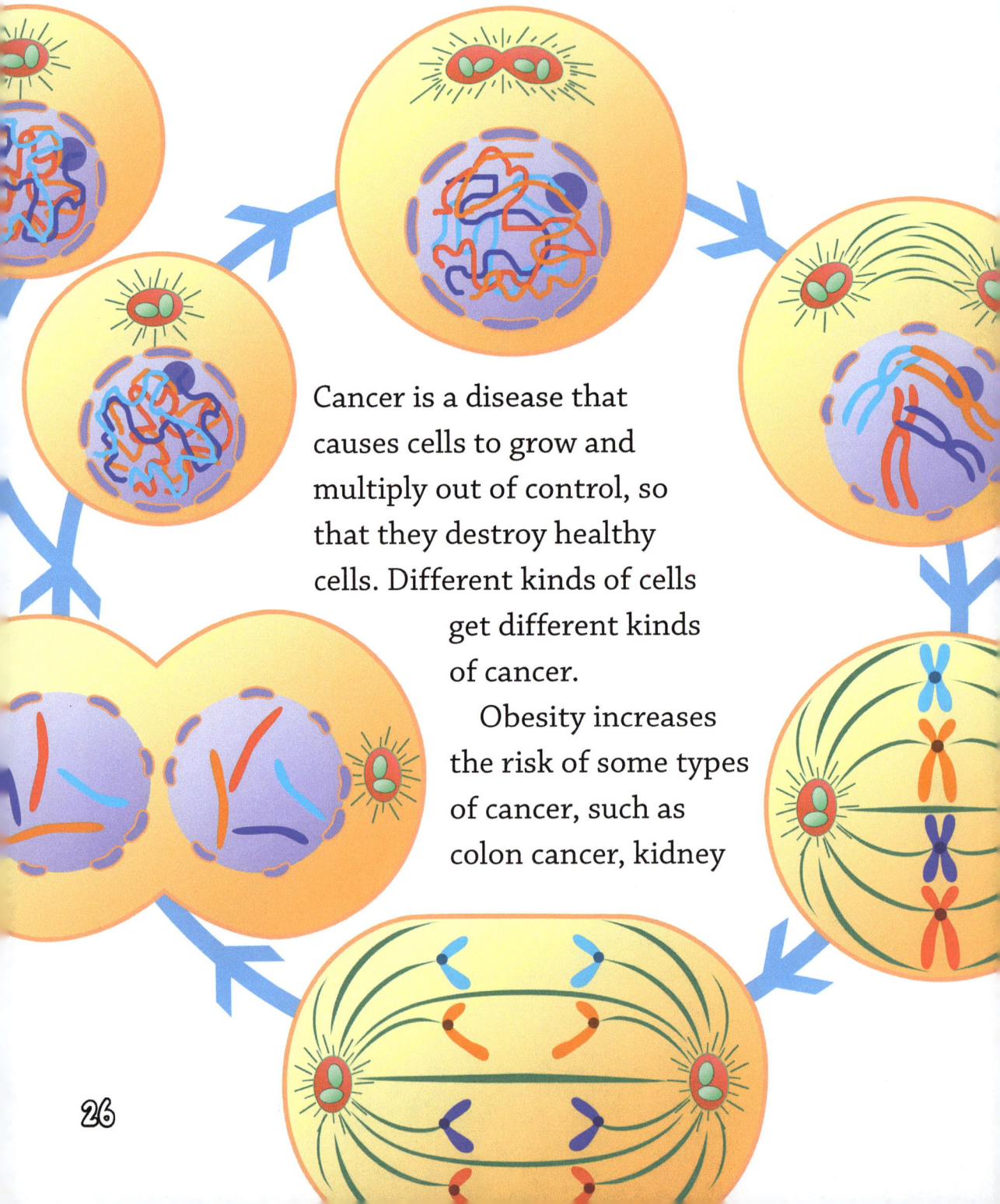

Cancer is a disease that causes cells to grow and multiply out of control, so that they destroy healthy cells. Different kinds of cells get different kinds of cancer.

Obesity increases the risk of some types of cancer, such as colon cancer, kidney cancer, and cancer of the esophagus (the tube between your mouth and your stomach). Doctors are studying whether obesity raises the risk for other types of cancer as well.

Not only does obesity increase the risk of cancer, but it makes it harder for you to heal, too. Obesity puts strain on your body, and cancer and treatments put even more strain on it. Doctors think people who are obese have more chance of dying from cancer than people whose weight is in the normal range.

Did You Know?

Almost all cancers caused by obesity happen in adults rather than children. But young people who are obese increase their risk of getting these cancers when they are still fairly young.

Your Emotions and Obesity

People who are obese are also more likely to have *depression*, *anxiety*, and *self-esteem* issues. Doctors don't know whether being obese leads to emotional issues, or whether being depressed or anxious leads to obesity. They think that it can work either way in different people.

Too often, people who are obese or overweight are teased and made fun of. Sometimes other people think that obese people are lazy or stupid or that it's their own fault that they are overweight. But that's not true!

Being teased or feeling bad about how you look can make you depressed. It can make you not want to spend time with other people.

On the other hand, if you are depressed or anxious, your body produces certain chemicals that make you gain weight faster.

Not everyone who is obese is depressed or anxious. People who are obese have the same range of emotions as everyone else does.

Words to Know

Depression: a disorder that causes extreme sadness and hopelessness, as well as trouble concentrating and doing things.

Anxiety: a sense of worry, nervousness, and an inability to relax.

Self-esteem: respecting yourself, feeling good about who you are.

What Causes Obesity?

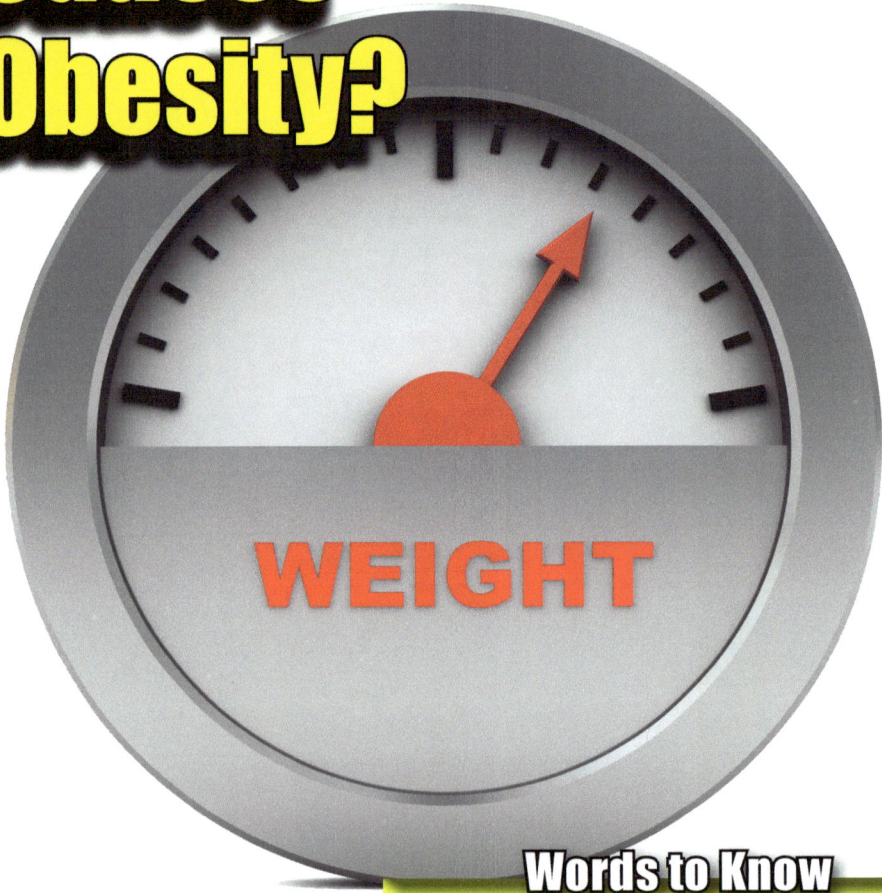

Taking in more *calories* than you use is what causes obesity. You take in calories through eating and drinking, and you use them by doing physical activity. Calories are the fuel your body uses to do all the things it needs to do. It's a little like the way a car burns gasoline to run.

Some people's bodies burn calories a lot faster than other people's, which means they can eat more food. When we say someone has a low metabolism, we mean that his body doesn't burn calories very quickly. He is more likely to gain weight than someone with a high metabolism.

Whether you have a high or low metabolism depends on a lot of things. Things like genetics—what your parents' metabolisms are like—how much sleep you get, and whether you are taking certain medicines can all have an effect. If you have a low metabolism, you will have to work harder to keep your weight in the normal range, but even people with high metabolisms can become obese.

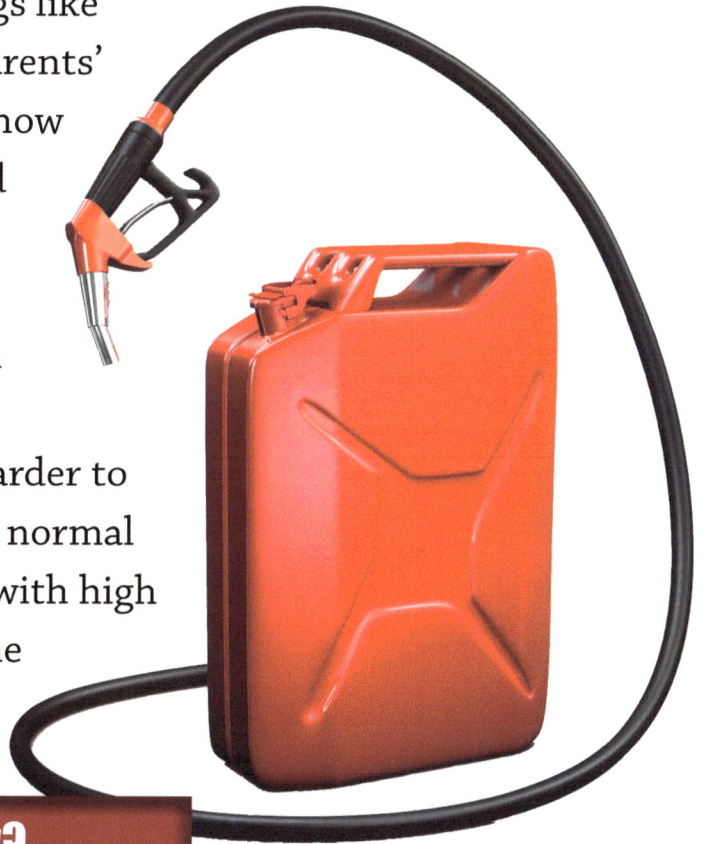

A Changing World

Life was different a hundred years ago, fifty years ago, or even twenty years ago. When your grandparents were kids, they probably didn't go out to eat very often. They probably didn't watch a lot of TV, and people didn't have computers at home.

Did You Know?

Hamburgers are bigger than they used to be. In fact, they're two to eight times bigger than a normal serving! When you eat a large cheeseburger, fries, and a soda, you could easily be eating as many calories in a single meal as you should eat in an entire day.

Instead, people worked hard. They also ran around and were active when they wanted to have fun. And they ate healthier, smaller meals.

Nowadays, both grownups and kids don't exercise as much as they once did. They spend most of their time sitting down. They eat more fat. They eat larger meals. And all those things help make more people overweight and obese.

33

Everyone is busy these days. Maybe you play sports or take music lessons or are in an after-school club. Your brothers and sisters are probably just as busy, too. And your parents are busy with their own lives and with making sure you get to all of your activities on time.

With all that busyness and running here and there, it's hard to eat right. *Packaged foods* are cheap, quick, and easy, but often not all that healthy.

Words to Know

Packaged foods: foods that have been dried, salted, or treated with chemicals so that they can be stored in boxes or in ready-to-heat portions in the freezer.

A fast food drive-through is even quicker, but probably even unhealthier. When everyone is tired from a long day at school, work, and after-school activities, grabbing a burger and fries on the way home can sound like a great idea. And while that's okay once in a while, doing it too often can be a very unhealthy habit. Finding ways to stay healthy when you're so busy takes a little more planning—but it's worth it! As a family, you can decide to make other choices.

Your Diet and You

The foods you eat change the way your body works. Some things taste delicious but don't give your body a lot of nutrients. Some things might make you feel happy while you are eating them—but then leave you feeling not so good later.

Most people naturally crave foods that are sweet, salty, or greasy. Scientists think this is because our ancestors needed more calories than they usually got. Sweet foods usually had more calories. People needed salt to make up for the salt they lost when they were sweating. And greasy foods usually had more protein. People who got these types of foods could survive longer than those who didn't. All that was great thousands of years ago when people had to work hard just to stay alive—but it isn't as helpful now, when food is more plentiful and our lives are easier.

Words to Know

Crave: to really want something.

Ancestors: our relatives who lived a long time ago.

Food and Feelings

Do you ever eat because you're sad? Do you eat when you get upset? Or do you want to eat certain kinds of food when you're sad or upset?

Food can shape our emotions. Certain foods, like chocolate or spicy foods, cause the body to produce endorphins. Endorphins are chemicals made in your brain that make you feel good. They are produced in order to help us deal with pain or stressful situations. So eating sweet food can make your body release endorphins and feel good for a little while. But our bodies usually process sugar very quickly. That means that the good feelings you got from eating the sweet food go away very quickly, too.

People sometimes eat food to make themselves feel better when they're sad or upset. But this doesn't work for very long, because it doesn't take care of the REASON you were sad or upset in the first place! Often the food people eat when they feel bad isn't very healthy. And that causes its own set of problems.

Choosing
What You Eat

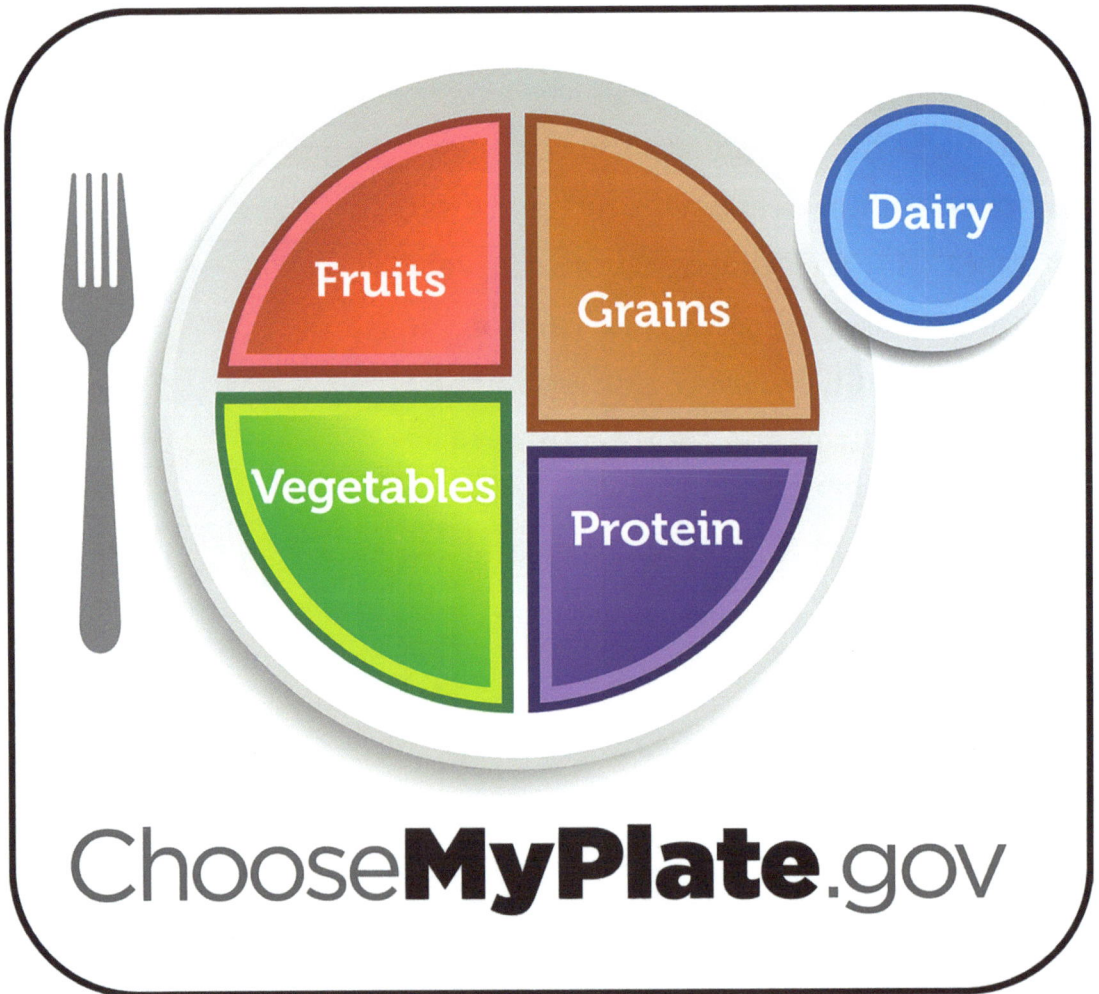

Every day, you can make choices about what you eat. Many countries' governments have developed a food pyramid or other chart that helps you make good decisions about the kinds of foods to eat and how much of them you need. The facing page shows an example—the United States Department of Agriculture's MyPlate. Most countries' diagrams have some things in common, such as emphasizing fruits and vegetables.

Start Moving!

Your body needs to move! Your muscles work best when they get to stretch and exercise. Your heart and lungs get stronger and work better when they work hard on a regular basis.

Doctors have discovered that regular exercise has lots and lots of benefits. Exercise keeps your body healthy and strong. Just as obesity raises your risk of diseases like cancer, diabetes, high blood pressure, and heart disease, keeping a healthy weight and exercising regularly lowers the risk of having those same problems.

There are lots of ways to get exercise. Go for a walk or a bike ride instead of staying inside after school. Run around on the playground. Fly a kite. Shoot some hoops with your friends. Kick a soccer ball. Put on some music and dance. The possibilities are endless!

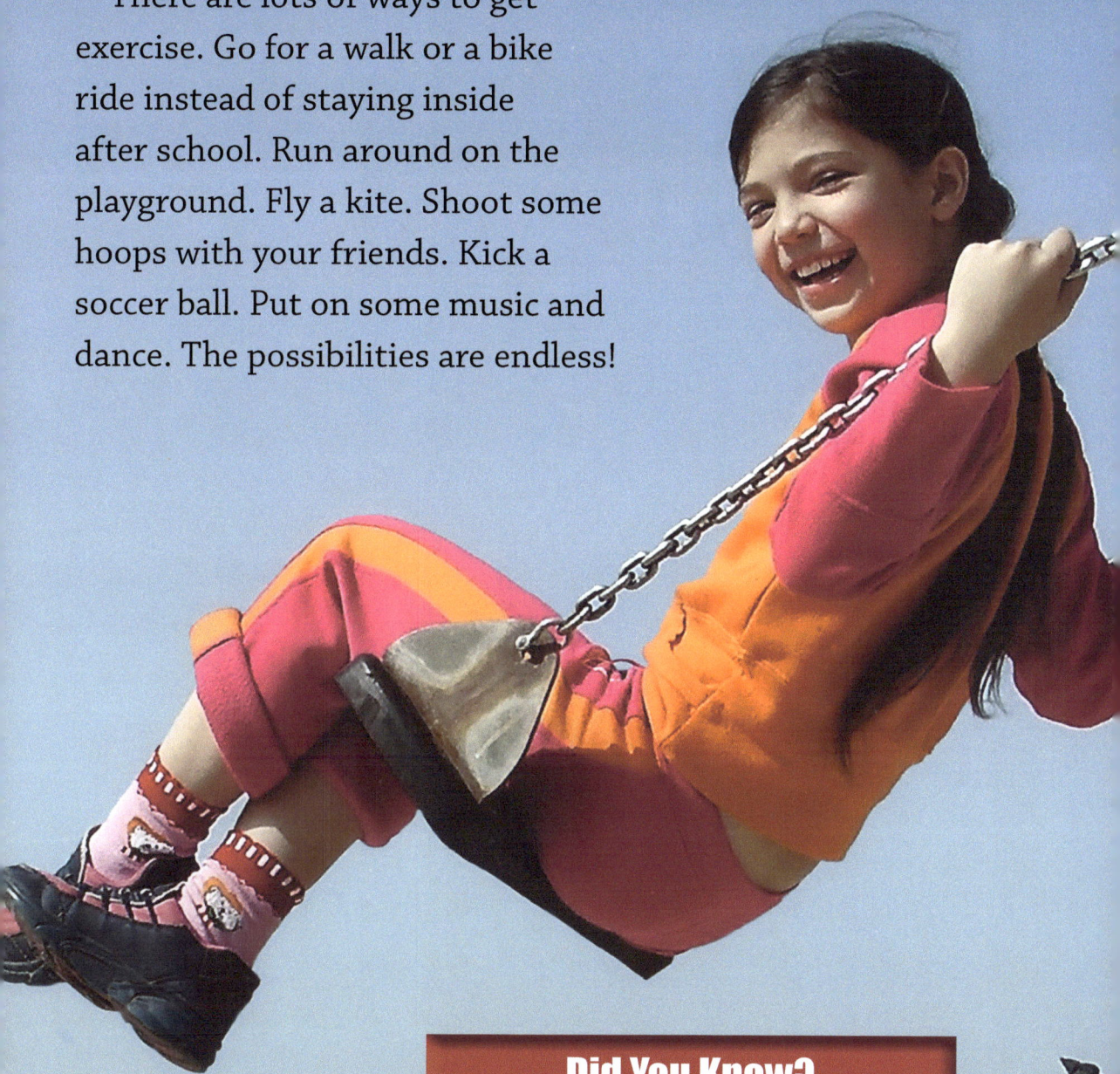

Did You Know?

Moving your body isn't just good for your heart, bones, and muscles. It's good for your mind and emotions, too! Doctors have found that people who exercise regularly are usually calmer, happier, and can deal with stress better.

43

Turn Off the TV and Your Computer!

Televisions and computers can be great things. You can learn things from television programs. You can enjoy a good movie or show. You can use a computer to research a school project. And then you can use it to create that project.

TURN IT OFF!

But too much time watching TV or playing on the computer isn't good for you. When you sit in front of a TV or computer for a long time, your body isn't moving much. You aren't burning very many calories. Doctors think kids should limit their "*screen time*" to no more than two hours a day. Instead, go outside! Do something active! Move!

Words to Know

Screen time: time you spend sitting in front of a TV or computer screen.

You and Your Family

Your family's way of life will shape your health. You might feel as though there's nothing you can do about that. Maybe your dad makes dinner every night, and your mom usually does the grocery shopping. Maybe you don't have a lot of say about what your family eats.

And what about your activities? Maybe every Sunday afternoon, you and your family go bike riding— or maybe instead, you all watch football on televison. There's nothing wrong with either of those activities. But one burns more calories than the other.

Your family's health and weight are shaped by the food and activities you enjoy. If your family usually sits still to have fun, maybe you could suggest doing something active. If you usually eat fast food after practice, suggest something healthier. You're a part of the family, too! And you can make a difference.

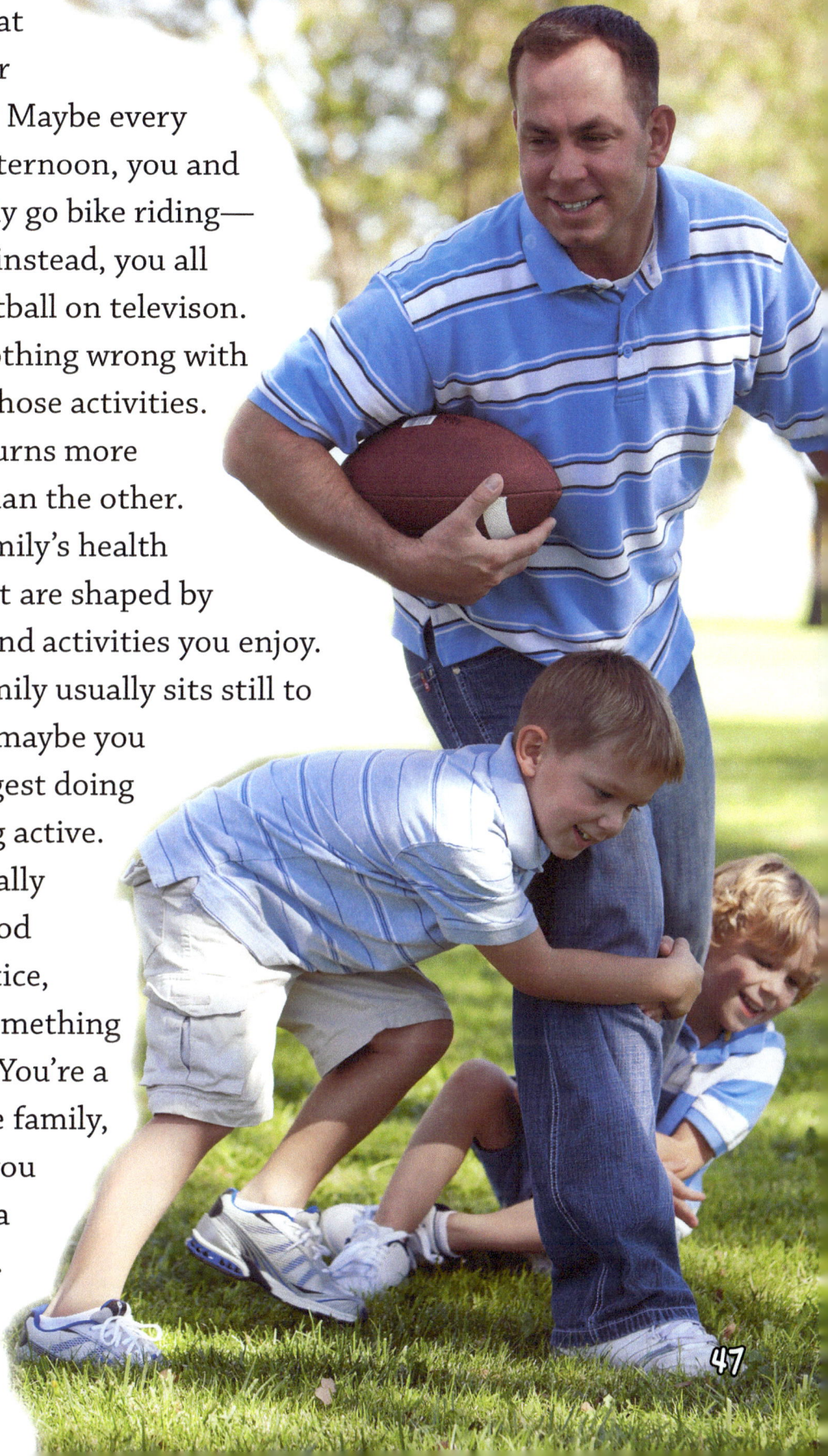

Research: Discovering New Facts About Obesity

Doctors and scientists have spent a lot of time studying obesity. They want to know why some people are more likely to be overweight than others. They want to know the best ways to help people stay at a healthy weight.

Lots of people think obesity is caused simply by people eating too much and not getting enough exercise. This is certainly part of the problem, but the causes of obesity are a lot more complicated than that. For example, you can *inherit* a *tendency* to be overweight from your parents. Lots and lots of different things can play a role in whether or not you are likely to be overweight!

Did You Know?

Missing two hours of sleep a night can make you 73 percent more likely to become obese.

Drinking fewer sweet drinks, like soda or sweetened juice, can help you better control your weight.

Some prescription medicines can make you gain or lose weight.

Doctors don't entirely understand this problem—but they're working on new ways to treat it. Scientists are even experimenting with an obesity vaccine. This means you could get a shot that would help keep you from becoming overweight!

Words to Know

Inherit: get something that is passed down to you by your parents.

Tendency: likelihood of moving in a certain direction.

What the World Is Doing About Obesity

Obesity is a problem everywhere in the world. Some people think that obesity is only a problem in richer countries. People in very poor countries can have trouble with obesity as well, though. Sometimes, people can be both undernourished and obese at the same time. That happens when people eat things with a lot of calories but not very many nutrients.

WHO (the World Health Organization) works with people to help them learn how to be healthier. Because WHO works with people all over the world, it deals with some people who are starving and don't have enough food—and it also deals with people who eat too much and eat the wrong kinds of food. WHO works with doctors, teachers, and other leaders to "make healthy choices easy choices." That means WHO tries to help people know the right choices to make about food and exercise, and then make it easier for people to choose those things.

Countries around the world are also doing things to help people make the right choices about food and activities. Education is very important. The more you know, the more you can change!

Words to Know

WHO: The World Health Organization is the part of the UN (United Nations) that is responsible for finding solutions to the world's health problems.

What Can You Do?

As a kid, it sometimes feels like a lot of things are out of your control. People tell you where to go and what to do. You don't have a choice about whether or not you go to school and what you learn while you're there. Sometimes, you might feel like you don't have any power at all. But that's not true!

Even if you can't make all the decisions about your life, there's a lot that you CAN decide. You can decide what you want for a snack. You can decide to turn off the computer and go outside and play. Most of all, you can decide that you want to be a happy and healthy person.

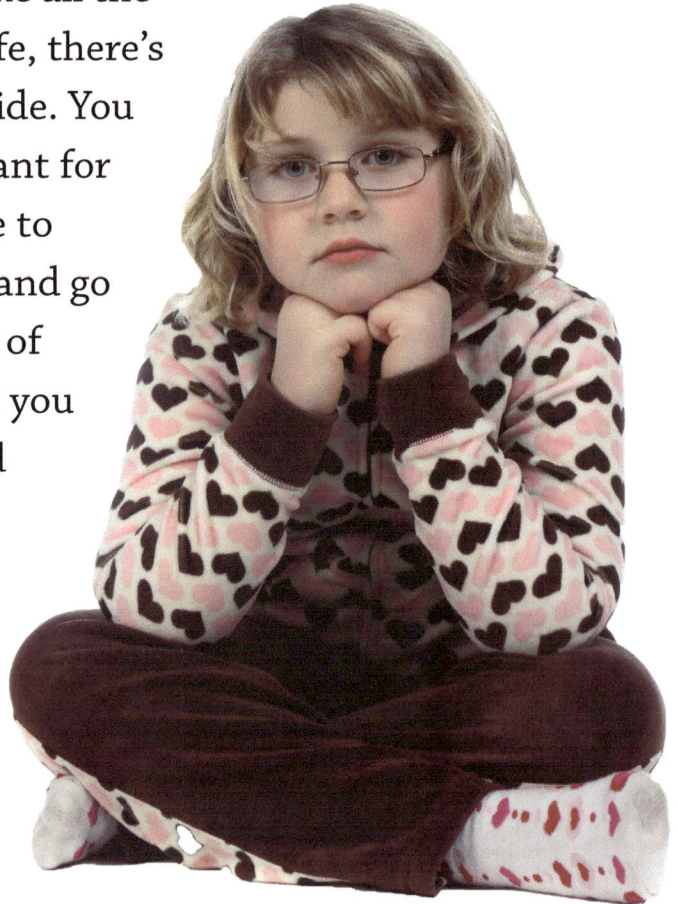

Michelle Obama, the *First Lady* of the United States, has a *campaign* called Let's Move! that fights childhood obesity. The website has five steps to help:

1. Move every day!
2. Try new fruits and veggies.
3. Drink lots of water.
4. Do jumping jacks to break up TV time.
5. Help make dinner.

Start taking charge of your life!

Obesity and Others

Sometimes, people aren't very nice to others who are obese. Sometimes, they don't know how to talk to overweight people, so they make fun of them or ignore them. Maybe you've done that to somebody yourself. Or maybe you are overweight or obese and you've had people ignore you or insult you because of it.

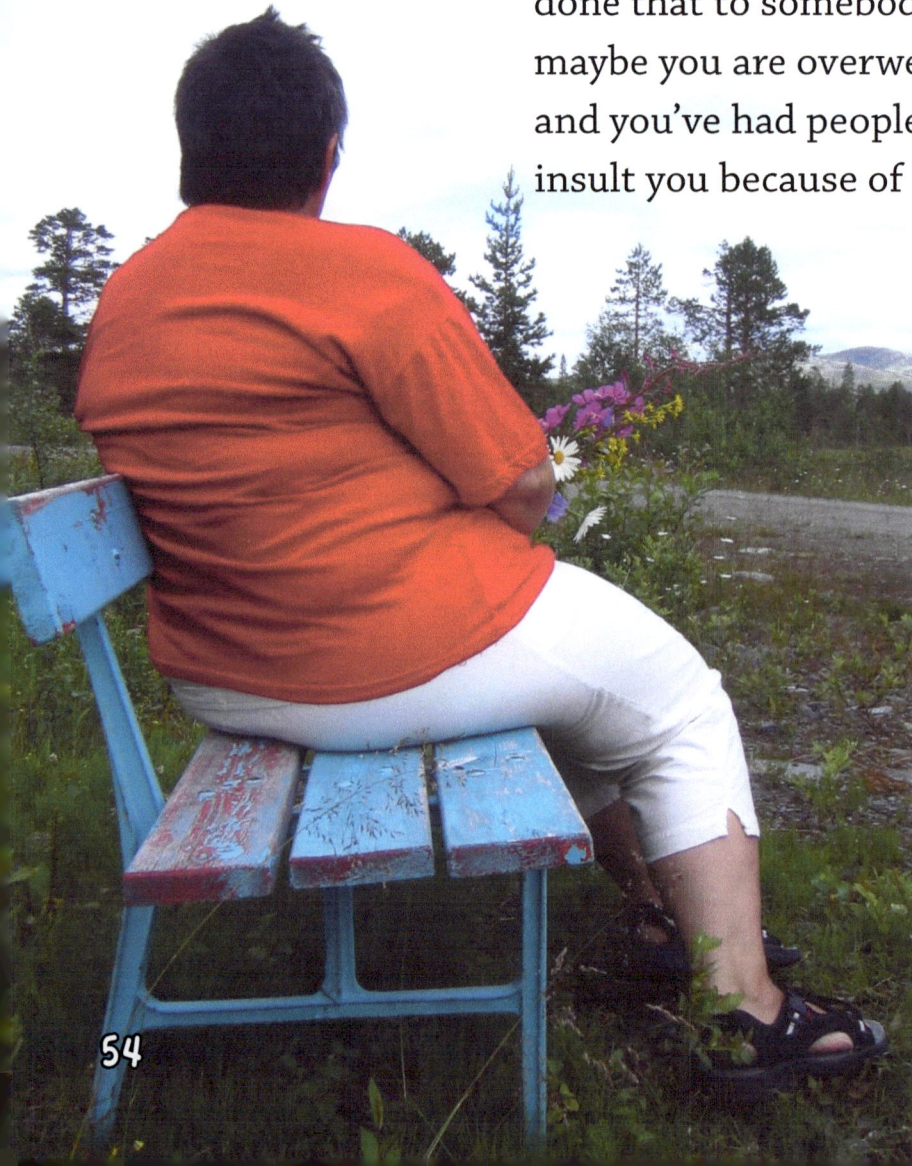

But overweight and obese people are just people. They're like everyone else. They have great things about them and they have problems. People sometimes have *stereotypes* about those who are overweight or obese, though. They think maybe they aren't as smart or as interesting as other people. The truth is, obesity has nothing to do with how smart or interesting a person is.

People who are obese or overweight are sometimes unhappy or lonely because of how others treat them. But people who are obese can be just as happy and popular as anyone else.

When you meet someone, don't let his weight change how you think of him. Look deeper and find out who he really is!

Words to Know

Stereotypes: ideas people have about a group of people. They are often insulting. And they're often wrong! People are individuals.

You're Worth It!

So what's the bottom line? Why should you bother to keep your body healthy with good food and exercise?

You should bother because you're worth it! You are an amazing person and you have a lot to offer. Your life will be happier and better if you take care of your body.

People come in all shapes and sizes. And there's nothing wrong with that! Healthy isn't about whether you are small or large.

Your body is an incredible thing. If you eat nutritious food, drink lots of water, get plenty of sleep, and make sure you move around a lot, your body will be healthy and strong.

You have an exciting life ahead of you. So make good choices now. Even if obesity is already a problem for you, you can decide you want to make a change. Your doctor and your parents can help you start making good decisions about what you eat and the activities you do. No matter what, your life can be amazing. Decide you want to be the best you can be—and go for it! You really are worth it!

Real Kids

When Chelsea was six, she started putting on weight. Before she was fourteen, she weighed over 210 pounds. Other kids teased her. She felt miserable, but she just kept eating more.

Then, her doctor told her about a program called SHINE (Self-Help, Independence, Nutrition, and Exercise).

At SHINE, Chelsea made new friends. She started eating better and being more active. In less than two years, she had lost over 70 pounds. She was healthier. She felt better about herself. "Everyone is proud, and I've impressed myself," she told the British paper *The Mirror*.

Find Out More

These books and websites will tell you more about HIV/AIDS, what you can do to protect yourself, and how you can help fight this disease.

Chilman-Blair, Kim and John Taddeo. *What's Up With Pam? Medikidz Explain Childhood Obesity.* New York: Rosen Central, 2010.

Hynson, Colin. *What Can We Do About Obesity?* London, U.K.: Franklin Watts, 2010.

Jimerson, N. M. *Childhood Obesity.* Farmington Hills, Mich.: Lucent Books, 2008.

Robbins, Lynette. *How to Deal With Obesity.* New York: PowerKids Press, 2009.

West, Linda Taylor. *Too Much.* Willow, Alaska: Little Britches Children's Books, 2008.

Action for Healthy Kids
www.actionforhealthykids.org

BAM! (Body and Mind)
www.bam.gov

Let's Move!
www.letsmove.gov

Nutrition Explorations: Kids
www.nutritionexplorations.org/kids/main.asp

What "Being Overweight" Means
kidshealth.org/kid/nutrition/weight/overweight.html

Index

Picture Credits

About the Author

Sheila Stewart has written many books for young adults and children. She lives with her family in New York State in the United States.

About the Consultant

Elise DeVore Berlan, MD, MPH, FAAP, is a faculty member of the Division of Adolescent Health at Nationwide Children's Hospital and an Assistant Professor of Clinical Pediatrics at the Ohio State University College of Medicine. She completed her fellowship in adolescent medicine at Children's Hospital Boston and obtained a master's degree in public health at the Harvard School of Public Health. Dr. Berlan completed her residency in pediatrics at the Children's Hospital of Philadelphia, where she also served an additional year as chief resident. She received her medical degree from the University of Iowa College of Medicine.